DE

$6.00

W9-AVB-997

6.7

PTS.
1.0

LET'S ROCK

FOSSILS

RICHARD AND LOUISE SPILSBURY

Chicago, Illinois

www.heinemannraintree.com
Visit our website to find out more information about Heinemann-Raintree books.

To order:

☎ Phone 888-454-2279

💻 Visit www.heinemannraintree.com to browse our catalog and order online.

Edited by Louise Galpine and Diyan Leake
Designed by Victoria Allen
Illustrated by Geoff Ward and KJA artists
Picture research by Hannah Taylor
Originated by Capstone Global Library Ltd
Printed and bound in the United States of America,
North Mankato, MN

14 13 12 11
10 9 8 7 6 5 4 3 2

Library of Congress Cataloging-in-Publication Data
Spilsbury, Louise.
  Fossils / Louise and Richard Spilsbury.
    p. cm. — (Let's rock)
  Includes bibliographical references and index.
  ISBN 978-1-4329-4682-1 (hb)
  ISBN 978-1-4329-4690-6 (pb)
  1. Fossils—Juvenile literature. I. Spilsbury, Richard, 1963– II.
Title.
  QE714.5.S644 2011
  560—dc22   2010022233

062011
006158RP

Acknowledgments
The author and publisher are grateful to the following for permission to reproduce copyright material: Alamy Images p. **11** (© Tom Bean); © Capstone Publishers pp. **28** (Karon Dubke), **29** (Karon Dubke); Corbis pp. **4** (epa/Wu Hong), **5** (Layne Kennedy), **15** (Xinhua Press/Xinhua/Xu Chaoyang), **23** (Science Faction/Louie Psihoyos), **25** (Science Faction/Louie Psihoyos); Florida Museum of Natural History p. **9** (Jason Bourque); Getty Images pp. **10** (AFP Photo), **16** (Howard Grey); Photolibrary pp. **6** (Reinhard Dirscherl), **7** (Gerald Hoberman), **13** (Oxford Scientific/Paul Kay), **17** (Peter Arnold Images/Fred Bruemmer), **20** (Britain on View/Joe Cornish), **21** (Robert Harding/C. Black), **22** (Enrique Algarra); Science Photo Library pp. **8** (Bernhard Edmaier), **27** (Dirk Wiersma).

Cover photograph of a dinosaur exhibition in Edmonton, Canada, reproduced with permission of Getty Images (Grant Faint).

We would like to thank Dr. Stuart Robinson for his invaluable help in the preparation of this book.

Every effort has been made to contact copyright holders of any material reproduced in this book. Any omissions will be rectified in subsequent printings if notice is given to the publisher.

Disclaimer
All the Internet addresses (URLs) given in this book were valid at the time of going to press. However, due to the dynamic nature of the Internet, some addresses may have changed, or sites may have changed or ceased to exist since publication. While the author and publisher regret any inconvenience this may cause readers, no responsibility for any such changes can be accepted by either the author or the publisher.

CONTENTS

Rock roles
Find out about the work involved in the study of rocks.

Science tip
Check out our smart tips to learn more about rocks.

Number crunching
Discover the amazing numbers in the world of rocks.

Biography
Read about people who have made important discoveries in the study of rocks.

Some words are printed in bold, **like this**. You can find out what they mean by looking in the glossary on page 30.

WHAT ARE FOSSILS?

Fossils are the remains of plants and animals that lived millions of years ago. These remains are usually **preserved** in rock.

Some fossils are of individual body parts, such as shells, teeth, and bones. Others are of complete bodies of trees and other living things. There are also many fossils of things animals left behind, such as droppings, eggs, and footprints.

Scientists use fossil bones to piece together full-size replicas of ancient animals such as dinosaurs.

Number crunching

It is possible that 99 percent of all the different types of animals that ever lived on Earth are **extinct**. The only way to find out about them is by examining fossils from rocks.

FASCINATING FOSSILS

For most of Earth's long history there were no written records, so fossils in rocks are very important clues to our planet's past. By studying fossils, we can find out about some of the plants and animals that lived long ago. For example, some fossil horse skeletons reveal that these animals were much smaller than today's horses, and that they had three toes rather than a single hoof on each leg.

Biography

In 1667 the Danish scientist Niels Stenson, or "Steno" (1638–1686), was examining a giant shark when he realized that its teeth looked like the triangular-shaped rocks people called tongue stones. Steno became the first person to explain how parts like teeth could change into fossils inside layers of rock, which themselves formed slowly over time.

By comparing fossil teeth to modern shark teeth, scientists figured out that the biggest ancient shark was over 12 meters (39 feet) long. That is about as long as a bus!

WHAT LIVING THINGS BECAME FOSSILS?

The first living things to become fossils were **bacteria**. Groups of these tiny creatures looked like slimy mats on the bubbling-hot oceans two billion years ago. By one billion years ago, there were also early plants called algae in shallow seas and on coasts.

THE FIRST SEA ANIMALS

The earliest sea animal fossils that have been found are from soft-bodied **invertebrates**, such as sponges, jellyfish, and sea worms, from 600 million years ago. Later, some invertebrates developed shells for protection. One of the most well known is the spiral-shelled **ammonoid**, which first appeared 415 million years ago. **Ammonites** are a suborder of ammonoid. The largest ammonite fossil ever found was 1.5 meters (5 feet) across. That is as big as a truck tire!

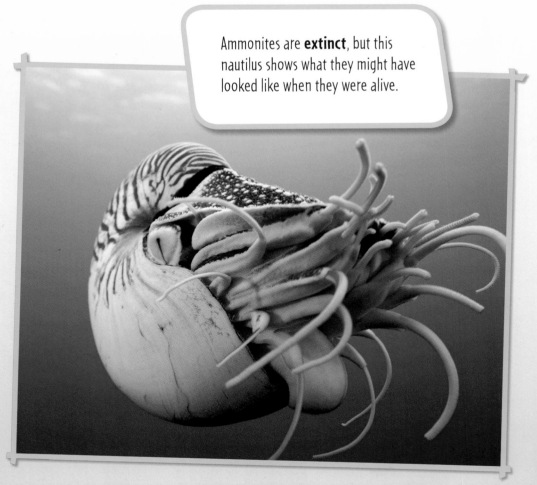

Ammonites are **extinct**, but this nautilus shows what they might have looked like when they were alive.

THE FIRST FISH

The first fish in the sea lived about 450 million years ago. They were worm-like creatures that sucked food from the seabed. Later there were bony fish with jaws and teeth. The *Dunkleosteus* lived nearly 380 million years ago. Fossils show that this monster was 10 meters (32 feet) long and its jagged, bony jaws gave it the strongest bite of any fish ever.

Rock roles

Paleontologists are time detectives. They find rocks that contain fossils and dig and explore sites. They also clean, repair, rebuild, and identify fossils all over the world.

In 1938 fishermen off the coast of South Africa caught such a strange-looking fish that they sent it to a museum. This **living fossil** was a coelacanth, a fish that paleontologists thought was extinct. It looks exactly the same as it did 360 million years ago.

JUNGLE LIFE

Plants began to grow on land around 400 million years ago. By 300 million years ago, there were hot, damp jungles. From leaf fossils found in rock, we can tell that some ancient ferns were 15 meters (nearly 50 feet) tall, and that plants related to the tiny mosses of today once stood about 40 meters (130 feet) high.

By looking at fossils in rocks from around the same time, we also know that many creatures lived in these jungles. There were small insects similar to those of today, such as beetles and flies. There were also millipedes 2 meters (6 feet) long scuttling along the forest floor and giant dragonflies flying in the air.

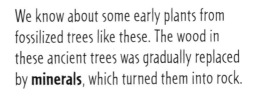

We know about some early plants from fossilized trees like these. The wood in these ancient trees was gradually replaced by **minerals**, which turned them into rock.

OUT OF THE WATER

Fossils of early land animals, such as *Ichthyostega*, suggest that they were related to fish. *Ichthyostega* had a head and tail like a fish, but legs for walking on land. One early **amphibian**, *Diplocaulus*, was particularly strange, as it had a triangular head. Later **reptiles** that lived on land, such as snakes, were like today's reptiles—but bigger. The biggest crocodile was 15 meters (50 feet) long.

Fossils of the biggest snake ever found suggest it was 13 meters (42 feet) long and weighed 1,135 kilograms (2,500 pounds)—making it longer than a bus and heavier than a car. Eeek!

Science tip

In the 1800s, people thought that the fossil heads of sea reptiles belonged to sea dragons! In fact, these were animals such as ichthyosaurs, which look similar to dolphins, and plesiosaurs, which had very long necks.

DINOSAURS

About 230 million years ago, a new group of reptiles **evolved**—the dinosaurs. Dinosaurs existed for 165 million years, and there were hundreds of different types. Some, such as *Diplodocus*, were enormous plant-eaters with long necks for reaching treetop leaves. *Ankylosaurus* was heavily armored with a sharp, club-shaped tail to fight off **predators**. *Tyrannosaurus rex* is one of the most famous dinosaur predators.

People are still making amazing dinosaur discoveries today, in places like this one in China. There are so many dinosaur fossils here that the area is known as "Dinosaur City."

Biography

O. C. Marsh (1831–1899) and E. D. Cope (1840–1897) were two U.S. dinosaur hunters. They became terrible enemies. Between them they found over 130 new types of dinosaurs, including an early type of tyrannosaur. However, they competed for these finds by lying, bribing, and cheating. They insulted each other in scientific journals (publications where research is discussed) and even destroyed each other's fossils.

BIRDS

The first birdlike fossil is 150 million years old, and it provides evidence of how birds developed. The archaeopteryx fossil skeleton has a tail, claws, and fingers like a reptile, but there are traces of feathers. These lead **paleontologists** to believe that modern birds are related to reptiles.

MAMMALS

The first **mammals** were small insect-eaters, rather like the shrews of today. They lived around 200 million years ago. From around 65 million years ago, many new mammals developed, such as horses, bats, whales, and **primates**. Some are still around today, but many, such as the saber-toothed tiger that lived around 10,000 years ago, have died out.

This archaeopteryx fossil was found in Germany and is 145 million years old. When alive, these birdlike animals were about the size of a crow.

HOW DID FOSSILS FORM?

Ammonites and a huge range of other creatures have been found in fossil form. But how did these fossils come about? Most fossils form over a very long time, as animals and plants are buried under mud and sand and slowly turn to rock.

TURNING TO ROCK

Most fossils were formed under the sea. For example, when a dead ammonite sank to the seabed, the soft parts of its body quickly rotted away. The shell was gradually buried in layers of sand or **sediment**. Over time, water seeped into the shell and **minerals** from the water replaced the minerals in the shell. Those minerals eventually turned to hard rock in exactly the shape of the ammonite shell, and a fossil was formed.

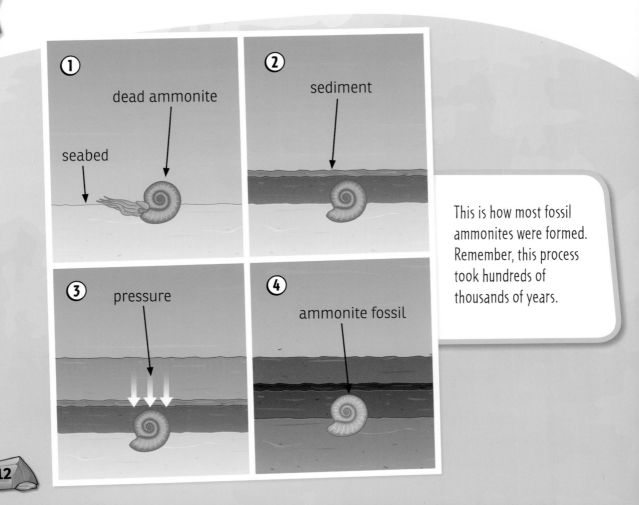

This is how most fossil ammonites were formed. Remember, this process took hundreds of thousands of years.

HARD FACTS

There are many ammonite fossils, but only a tiny percentage of the huge number of other ancient animals became fossils. A number of things stop a fossil from forming. Animals without bones quickly rot away, leaving no hard parts to become fossils. Dead remains will rot or be eaten by animals if they are not buried in sediment fairly quickly. Some remains are damaged as sediment piles up. For example, bird bones are light and fragile and usually crumble before they become fossils.

Number crunching
Today, there are about 300 types of octopus, but only 5 octopus fossils have ever been found.

Most fossils that we find are of sea animals that had shells. This ammonite's shell was replaced by a mineral that makes it look metallic.

TRACE FOSSILS

Trace fossils are traces that **prehistoric** animals left behind, such as footprints, eggs, droppings, and burrows. Trace fossils form in a similar way to other rock fossils. For example, when a dinosaur's footprints were buried under sand or mud, they hardened and became fossils as they turned into rock. Trails left by soft-bodied animals may be the only record we have that they existed.

Science tip

When you are at a beach or walking on mud, try making a trail. Think about how an ancient animal moved. How far apart would its footprints have been? If your traces are left undisturbed, they might become fossils in millions of years, too!

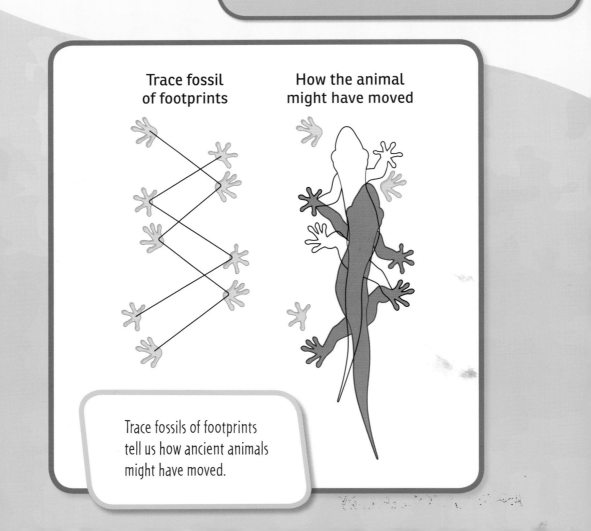

Trace fossil of footprints

How the animal might have moved

Trace fossils of footprints tell us how ancient animals might have moved.

SNAPSHOTS OF LIFE

Trace fossils are exciting because they tell us how ancient animals lived. For example, remains such as seeds or bones in fossil droppings show what animals ate. Fossil burrows reveal the routes that animals, such as worms, took as they searched for food. Trace fossils are also easier to find because one animal can leave many traces throughout its lifetime.

Biography

In the 1970s, U.S. paleontologist Jack Horner (born 1946) found a dinosaur nest site in Montana with fossil eggs, babies, and adult dinosaurs all around. This proved that some dinosaurs lived in groups and cared for their young together. We see this caring side to dinosaurs in the movie *Jurassic Park* because Horner advised the filmmakers.

These dinosaur egg fossils were found by workers at a construction site in China in 2009.

UNUSUAL FOSSILS

Fossils such as ammonites are animal remains turned into rock. Some fossils are actual ancient animals themselves. The **resin** of the pine tree is very sticky. When it oozes down the tree trunk, it can sometimes trap insects, spiders, or even frogs. As the resin continues to drip, it eventually covers the animal completely. When the resin dries up and hardens, it becomes amber. Animals that were trapped inside resin thousands of years ago have been perfectly **preserved** in amber. Today, **paleontologists** can study these fossils.

Science tip

If someone you know has amber jewelry, take a magnifying glass and see if you can see any tiny remains of ancient insects inside.

Some insect fossils are so well preserved in amber that you can see every detail, from their tiny eyes to the hairs on their legs.

TRAPPED IN TAR

In La Brea, California, there are pits of thick, black tar where paleontologists have found bones of **extinct** animals such as saber-toothed tigers. These were huge cats with teeth 17 centimeters (nearly 7 inches) long. When the animals stepped into these pools of natural oil, they quickly became stuck and sank into the tar, which perfectly preserved their bones.

FROZEN IN TIME

Fossils of whole woolly mammoths have been found in the cold region of Siberia, in northern Asia. These animals fell through thin ice, died in freezing water, and then froze solid. Thousands of years later, their remains were found. They had been preserved by ice, rather than turned to stone like other fossils.

The mammoth's shaggy hair kept it warm during the periods when much of the world was covered in ice.

WHERE DO WE FIND FOSSILS?

People find fossils all over the world, but there are sometimes surprises. For example, fossils of plants and animals that usually lived in hot places are found in places that are cold today. One reason for this is that the climate changed in different places on Earth. Another reason is land movement.

LAND ON THE MOVE

The rock that forms Earth's surface is called the **crust**. This crust has cracked in places to form enormous pieces called **tectonic plates**. The plates of the crust float on a thick layer of hot rock called the **mantle**. The mantle moves very slowly, and over millions of years it has moved the **continents** and the fossils inside them.

Fossils prove that trees and ferns grew in Antarctica 235 million years ago. Then, the climate changed, the continents shifted, and Antarctica moved over the South Pole.

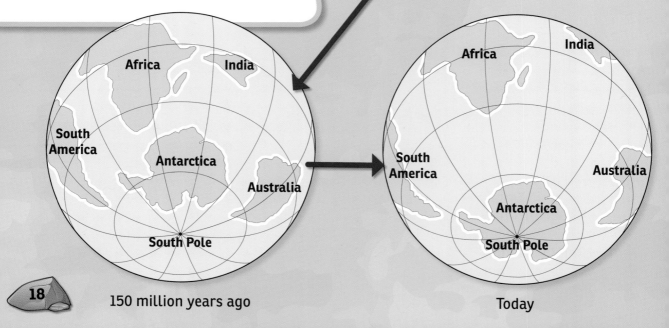

235 million years ago

150 million years ago

Today

WHERE ARE AMMONITES FOUND?

Another surprise is that **paleontologists** have found many fossils of **ammonites** and other sea animals at the top of the Himalayas, the highest mountains on Earth. The rocks where these fossils were formed were once under an ocean. Then, tectonic plates pushed against each other, and some parts of the crust were forced upward. This formed mountains, lifting rocks from the seabed high above sea level.

Number crunching

Ammonites are found in rocks in all sorts of places. This is because they spent millions of years (from about 415 million to 65 million years ago) swimming in oceans all over the world.

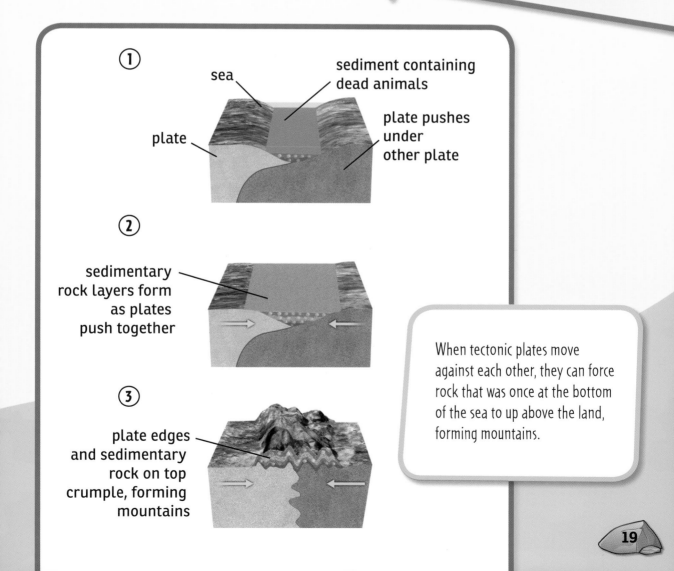

① sea
sediment containing dead animals
plate
plate pushes under other plate

② sedimentary rock layers form as plates push together

③ plate edges and sedimentary rock on top crumple, forming mountains

When tectonic plates move against each other, they can force rock that was once at the bottom of the sea to up above the land, forming mountains.

COMING TO THE SURFACE

Fossils may be everywhere, but if most were buried deep inside rocks, how do people find them? People sometimes find ammonites and other fossils when a **quarry** or a mine is dug, but it is the process of **weathering** that brings most fossils to the surface.

Weathering is the way that rocks on Earth's surface are constantly worn away by wind, rain, and ice. For example, water that gets into cracks in rock expands if it freezes. As it gets bigger, ice forces apart the grains of **minerals** that make up rocks. The loose pieces of rock that break off are washed away by rain, wind, and water. This is called **erosion**.

Over millions of years, weathering and erosion wear away rocks to reveal ammonites and other fossils that were once far below the surface.

THE RIGHT ROCKS

To find ammonites and most other fossils, you should look in **sedimentary rocks**. Sedimentary rocks form from layers of **sediment**. Over millions of years, upper layers crush lower layers, squeezing out water until layers become cemented together as rock.

THE ROCK CYCLE

All rocks on Earth, including sedimentary rock, are constantly changing in the **rock cycle**. Igneous rock forms from **magma** that comes out of **volcanoes** as a hot liquid. Through weathering and erosion, igneous rock breaks down into sediment, which eventually forms sedimentary rock. When deep layers of sedimentary rock are heated by magma and compressed by other rock layers, they change into metamorphic rock. Under extreme heat, the metamorphic rock melts. Then, the rock cycle begins again.

Most fossils are found in sedimentary rock like this.

HOW DO PEOPLE IDENTIFY FOSSILS?

The rock crumbles away and the outline of a fossil is revealed. What kind of animal have you found?

One way to identify the fossils you find is to compare them with pictures of similar fossils in books or on the Internet. You can also compare your finds with living things to see what similarities and differences there are. When **paleontologists** find a new fossil, they can name it themselves. For example, a **primate** fossil called "Ida" was named after a paleontologist's daughter.

If you found a fossil, how would you identify it?

Biography

Mary Anning (1799–1847) became a fossil hunter to earn money after her father died. She would rush out after storms that caused land to slide away and expose new fossils. Mary sold hundreds of fossils, including the first *Ichthyosaurus*. The well-known tongue-twister "She sells seashells by the seashore" was inspired by Mary Anning.

FAKE FOSSILS

Paleontologists also have to learn how to identify fake fossils. Some people make fake fossils by piecing bits of different fossils together or by mixing glue and ground rock from other fossils to replace missing pieces. In 1953 a famous fossil of an ape that was a bit like a human was proved to be an old human skull glued onto an orangutan's jaw. No one knows whether Charles Dawson, who found the fossil in 1912, was responsible—or whether he was the victim of the hoax.

Rock roles

Some paleontologists check that fossils brought to museums are not clever fakes. They use special **X-ray** equipment to see inside fossils and spot where pieces are joined together.

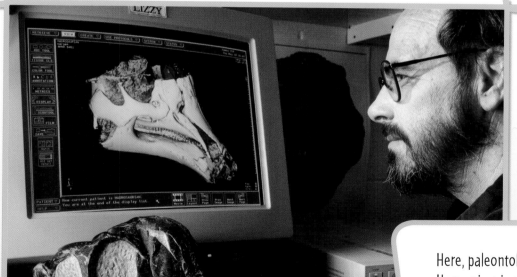

Here, paleontologist Jack Horner is using a special kind of X-ray machine to study a fossil skull.

DATING FOSSILS

To find out how old a fossil is, you could use **index fossils**. These are fossils from known periods of time that are found around the world.

Ammonoids make good index fossils because there were different types with different shell patterns. Each type lived during a certain time. So, if you find an ammonoid fossil from a certain time, you know that the rock you found it in, and any other fossils in that rock, are roughly the same age.

These are some of the ammonoids people use as index fossils.

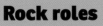

Rock roles

Some types of **element** change to another element over time at a fixed rate through a process called radioactive decay. By measuring how much of each element is in a rock, it is possible to calculate the age of the rock and the fossil inside it. This calculation is called radiometric dating.

Ammonoid index fossils

Goniatitina
When it lived:
395–225 million years ago

Ceratitina
When it lived:
280–190 million years ago

Ammonitina
When it lived:
190–65 million years ago

BECOME A FOSSIL HUNTER

Beaches at the base of cliffs and **quarries** are good places to look for fossils. Go with an adult or an organized tour. Wear a hard hat under cliffs and always wear safety goggles if you use a geological hammer to hit and split rocks.

When you find a fossil, draw a simple map of where you found it. Note which kind of rock the fossil is in and what other fossils are nearby. Take rock and fossil identification guides to help you identify your finds.

Science tip

To spot **sedimentary rock**, look for rock with horizontal layers, or bands, of different colors. Then scratch the rock with something hard. You can usually scrape marks into sedimentary rocks, and most also crumble easily.

Fossil hunters use a variety of hammers and other tools when they are on a major dig.

HOW DO WE USE FOSSILS?

We use fossils to date rocks and learn about Earth's history, but also to power cars and computers. Most of the energy we use for electricity and transportation is made from the fossil fuels coal, oil, and gas.

Coal was formed from ancient plants that sank into mud. The layers of mud hardened into rock that crushed the plant remains. Heat inside Earth changed the remains into black coal. Oil and gas were formed in a similar way, but mostly from **plankton** and sea animals that sank into sand.

Rock roles

Oil **geologists** study fossils to find oil. Certain tiny **index fossils** are only found in deep rock that also contains (or is above) rock that contains oil. Geologists know oil is near when they find these "microfossils."

These pie charts show how we use different types of fossil fuels.

15.7% 19.9% 6.6% 57.8%

oil

49.5% 45.3% 5.2%

gas

2.4% 1.0% 20.5% 76.1%

coal

industry   non-energy   transportation   other

PROBLEMS WITH FOSSIL FUELS

Fossil fuels took millions of years to form, but we are using them up very quickly. When they run out, there will not be any more.

Burning fossil fuels puts gases into the air that contribute to **global warming**, which is changing the world's climates. Many people say we should use more **renewable** sources of energy, such as solar (Sun) power, instead of fossil fuels.

Number crunching

If we continue using fossil fuels at the rate we do today, oil may run out in less than 40 years and gas in 50 to 150 years. Coal may run out within 1,000 years. Then what will people use to run their cars and make electricity?

Some coal has imprints of the leaves from which it was formed.

MAKE A TRACE FOSSIL!

Some **trace fossils** form when a shape, such as a footprint, is pressed into soft mud. The shape fills up with **sediments** such as mud, sand, or ash from **volcanoes**, and then hardens into rock in the shape of the print.

YOU WILL NEED:
- modeling clay
- an empty margarine tub
- vegetable oil
- plaster of Paris
- water
- a mixing bowl
- shells and/or a plastic model dinosaur.

WHAT TO DO:

1. Roll out a flat slab of modeling clay the size of the margarine tub. Put the modeling clay into the bottom of the tub.

2. Press your shells or the feet of the plastic dinosaur firmly into the modeling clay, so that when you take them out again they leave an impression. Apply a small amount of vegetable oil to the impression surface to make it nonstick.

Mix plaster of Paris with water in the mixing bowl. Pour this into the margarine tub to cover the modeling clay. This acts like the sediment and water that filled impressions in the past. Tap gently on the sides of the tub to level the plaster and to remove any air bubbles.

4 Put the tub somewhere cool and let the plaster dry for a day or two, until it hardens.

5 When it is hard and completely dry, turn the tub upside down and empty it. Then peel away the modeling clay from the plaster-of-Paris "rock." You should be able to see your trace fossil in the rock.

GLOSSARY

ammonite member of a suborder of ammonoid that lived around 190–65 million years ago

ammonoid extinct creature that had a spiral shell. The oldest ammonoids lived 415 million years ago.

amphibian animal that can live on land and in water, such as a frog

bacteria simple and tiny living things that live in water, air, soil, and other living things

continent one of the large landmasses of Earth, such as Europe, Africa, or Asia

crust hard, rocky surface layer of Earth

element simplest chemical substance

erosion wearing away of rocks by flowing water, wind, and glaciers

evolve when a plant or animal develops and gradually changes from one form to another

extinct when a type of plant or animal dies out completely and no longer exists

geologist scientist who studies the rocks and soil from which Earth is made

global warming way that the temperature on parts of Earth is getting higher

index fossil fossil of a plant or animal known to have lived in a particular time

invertebrate animal without a backbone

living fossil living thing that is the same as something that is otherwise only known from fossils

magma molten rock below Earth's crust

mammal animal that gives birth to live babies (instead of laying eggs) and can feed its young on milk from its body

mantle very deep layer of hot rock below Earth's crust

mineral substance that is naturally present in Earth, such as gold and salt

paleontologist scientist who studies prehistoric life

plankton microscopic plants and animals that float on the surface of the ocean

predator animal that hunts, catches, and eats other animals

prehistoric time in history before information was written down

preserved kept in the same state or condition for a very long time

primate group of mammals that includes humans, monkeys, and apes

quarry place where large amounts of rock are dug out of the ground

renewable type of energy that is replaced naturally so it will not run out

reptile animal with scaly skin that lays eggs protected by a shell

resin sticky substance produced by some trees

rock cycle constant formation, destruction, and recycling of rocks through Earth's crust

sediment layer of very tiny pieces of rock or shells, such as sand or mud

sedimentary rock rock made when tiny pieces of rock or the skeletons or shells of sea animals are buried underground and compressed

tectonic plate one of the giant pieces that Earth's crust is cracked into

trace fossil traces that prehistoric animals left behind, such as footprints, droppings, eggs, and burrows

volcano opening in Earth's surface where magma escapes from underground

weathering breaking up of rock by weather conditions such as extremes of temperature

X-ray type of light that can pass through objects and make it possible to see inside them

FIND OUT MORE

BOOKS

Faulkner, Rebecca. *Fossils* (Geology Rocks!). Chicago: Raintree, 2008.

Graham, Ian. *Fossil Fuels* (Earth's Precious Resources). Chicago: Heinemann Library, 2005.

Pipe, Jim. *Earth's Rocks and Fossils* (Planet Earth). Pleasantville, N.Y.: Gareth Stevens, 2008.

WEBSITES

Learn all about fossils at this website, which includes a map of good places to find fossils:
www.fossilsforkids.com

Learn how to be a fossil hunter at this website:
www.sdnhm.org/kids/fossils/index.html

PLACES TO VISIT

American Museum of Natural History
Central Park West at 79th Street
New York, New York, 10024-5192
Tel: (212) 769-5100
www.amnh.org
Visit the museum's huge collection of fossils, which includes dinosaurs.

The Field Museum
1400 S. Lake Shore Drive
Chicago, Illinois 60605-2496
Tel: (312) 922-9410
www.fieldmuseum.org
Check out exhibits of fossils, including "Sue" the *Tyrannosaurus rex*.

INDEX